21st Century
Basic Skills
Library

TORNADOES!

by Cecilia Minden, PhD

Cherry Lake Publishing • Ann Arbor, Michigan

Published in the United States of America
by Cherry Lake Publishing
Ann Arbor, Michigan
www.cherrylakepublishing.com

Photo Credits: Cover and page 1, ©Gregor Kervina/Shutterstock, Inc.;
page 4, ©Steve Bloom Images/Alamy; page 6, ©Zastol'skiy Victor
Leonidovich/Shutterstock, Inc.; page 8, ©Dave Chapman/Alamy;
page 10, ©iStockphoto.com/clintspencer; page 12, ©Delmas Lehman/
Shutterstock, Inc.; page 14, ©Rob Marmion/Shutterstock, Inc.; page 16,
©PhotoStock-Israel/Alamy; page 18, ©Denise Mondloch; page 20,
©Ron Buskirk/Alamy

Library of Congress Cataloging-in-Publication Data
Minden, Cecilia.
  Tornadoes!/by Cecilia Minden.
    p. cm.—(21st century basic skills library level 2)
  Includes bibliographical references and index.
  ISBN-13: 978-1-60279-863-2 (lib. bdg.)
  ISBN-10: 1-60279-863-X (lib. bdg.)
  1. Tornadoes—Juvenile literature. I. Title. II. Series.
  QC955.2.M56 2010
  551.55'3—dc22   2009048577

Cherry Lake Publishing would like to acknowledge
the work of The Partnership for 21st Century Skills.
Please visit www.21stcenturyskills.org for more information.

Printed in the United States of America
Corporate Graphics Inc.
July 2010
CLFA07

TABLE OF CONTENTS

It's a Tornado!

What is that in the sky?

It's a **tornado**!

How does a tornado happen?

What can you do?

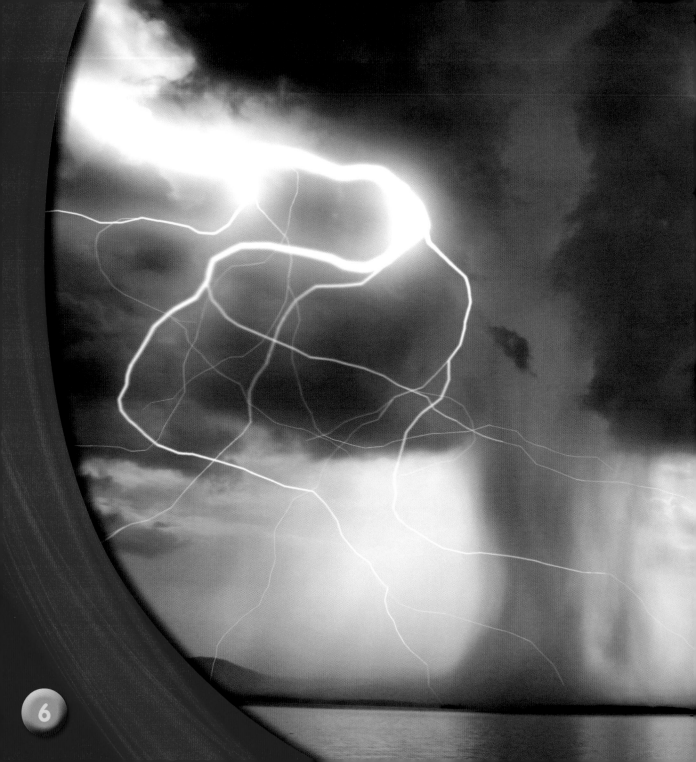

6

How Do Tornadoes Happen?

Warm, wet air meets cooler air.

Then there is a thunderstorm.

8

There may be a lot of rain and **hail**.

Sometimes a **funnel** drops from the storm clouds.

The funnel may touch the ground.

Then it is a tornado!

A tornado can move many miles per hour!

It will **damage** everything in its path.

What Can You Do?

Help your family make a plan.

Listen to **updates** about the weather.

A *watch* means there may be a tornado.

A tornado *warning* means you should find **shelter!**

Go to an inside hallway or bathroom.

Cover your head!

Soon the tornado will be over.

You can come out.

Be careful where you walk!

Find Out More

BOOK

Gibbons, Gail. *Tornadoes*. New York: Holiday House, 2009.

WEB SITE

FEMA for Kids—Tornadoes
www.fema.gov/kids/tornado.htm
Watch a tornado video and learn more about tornadoes.

Glossary

damage (DAM-ij) to harm something

funnel (FUHN-uhl) an open cone shape that narrows to a tube

hail (HAYL) lumps or balls of ice that fall from the sky during a storm

shelter (SHEL-tur) a place to stay safe and protected from danger

tornado (tor-NAY-doh) a whirling column of air that appears as a dark funnel-shaped cloud

updates (UP-dayts) the latest information about something

Home and School Connection

Use this list of words from the book to help your child become a better reader. Word games and writing activities can help beginning readers reinforce literacy skills.

a	everything	it	per	touch
about	family	its	plan	updates
air	find	it's	rain	walk
an	from	listen	shelter	warm
and	funnel	lot	should	warning
bathroom	go	make	sky	watch
be	ground	many	sometimes	weather
can	hail	may	soon	wet
careful	hallway	means	storm	what
clouds	happen	meets	that	where
come	head	miles	the	will
cooler	help	move	then	you
cover	hour	of	there	your
damage	how	or	thunderstorm	
do	in	out	to	
does	inside	over	tornado	
drops	is	path	tornadoes	

Index

About the Author

Cecilia Minden is the former Director of the Language and Literacy Program at the Harvard Graduate School of Education. She currently works as a literacy consultant for school and library publishers and is the author of more than 100 books for children.